Does this sound familiar? You are asked to lead a change program. Perhaps you are a member of the team, a manager, an HR professional, or an external training partner (what, for simplicity's sake, we will refer to as a "change agent" in this issue of TD at Work). You've discovered a great training tool or model that fits the organization's needs perfectly, and you have a vested interest in the program's delivery and subsequent success.

Initial impressions are that the program has been a huge success. The participants gain insights, know what changes need to take place, and have practiced the associated new skills and behavior. Three months later during the evaluation, you realize the learning was never really transferred to the job. Change didn't take place as quickly or as thoroughly as desired or expected. So, you're facing a big disappointment and maybe a major waste of time, energy, and money.

Effective learning and development models, and the concepts behind them, can only be successfully taken onboard if we understand human behavior. Cognitive behavior psychology shows us that even people who genuinely want to change find it difficult. As Simon Sinek explains in *Leaders Eat Last*, brain science confirms that people need to feel involved in driving the change, rather than being threatened by it.

Our C Step program—which has origins in Parenting With Love and Limits, an evidence-based treatment model for families, focuses on people, not just learning plans.

In this TD at Work you will learn:
- why behavior change doesn't always happen
- the three major blockers preventing change
- steps you can take to ensure the best chance of success with changing behavior.

EVEN THOUGH INDIVIDUALS WANT TO CHANGE, THEY FIND IT HARD TO DO SO AND DON'T UNDERSTAND WHY.

WHY CAN'T WE CHANGE?

We have seen in our work that, when planning change, many organizations focus on the plan and not the people. The psychological aspects of change are not addressed, decisions are made in the boardroom and not on the work floor, and there is a noticeable lack of follow-up and feedback. All of which means that, even though individuals want to change, they find it hard to do so and don't understand why.

Often, change plans are too complex and inconsistent. Effort and money is invested in new systems and initiatives that don't succeed. Employees are trained in new techniques and expected to adopt the behaviors needed for an organizational change. But the human factor is not taken into account. We tend to be too optimistic and assume that if participants seem to be willing and able to change, they will.

The reality is that we don't always do the things we want to do. We all know we shouldn't wait until the last minute to finish a project, just as we all know we should visit our aging aunt, go to the gym, or organize our office. We know we *should* do these things. However, it is just not feasible for a human being to fulfill all of these social demands and requirements. We are not robots.

The good news is that the neuroplasticity of the human brain allows for change. The bad news is that our brain prefers homeostasis and longs for what it knows best. Many of your employees are already sufficiently self-aware to know where their opportunities for improvement lie and which pitfalls to avoid. But too often, training sessions are focused on the superficial aspects of behavior change.

In addition, there is little attention given to understanding the existing behavior and how employees have benefited from it. People do not understand why they are there. This understanding is necessary before starting to change anything.

In the past decade, there has been a substantial amount of research about behavior change. People have the tendency to hold on to their attitudes, traits, and behaviors even when (or especially when) their managers try to convince them otherwise. For many people, change brings feelings of uncertainty, stress, and a lack of control (Stoffer 2002; Weeks, Roberts, Chonko, and Jones 2004). This means that the prefrontal cortex of their brain underperforms, and they fall back on earlier behavioral patterns and habits (Duhigg 2012).

Awareness of common change blockers and how to deal with them will help you make change happen more efficiently and with longer-lasting results.

Resistance to Change

Change blockers are the part of us that make us resist change and limit our abilities to embrace it. They are emotional strategies that we've developed over time to avoid pain and discomfort. The result of these blockers is that we often won't or can't take on sufficient responsibility to develop ourselves (or members of our team).

These patterns may involve both fear of change in general and fear of specific negative consequences that a certain kind of change can

CHANGE BLOCKERS: POSITIVES AND NEGATIVES

Change blockers get in our way when we intend to change behavior. These emotional strategies protect us from the discomfort we may experience during a change. Our brain may know change would be beneficial, but it cannot easily overcome these hurdles. By understanding the positive and negative aspects of change blockers, we can work with them.

Change Blocker	Positive	Negative
Fear	• Prevents us from taking dangerous risks. • Encourages us to build our skills to overcome these obstacles. • Gives us strong physical warning signals. • Without this change blocker, we would make hasty decisions.	• Fear often takes over and, before we know it, we become cowards. • We start to fear small things that are not dangerous at all. • It can become paralyzing. • When we don't challenge this change blocker, we may develop an avoidance strategy and never step out of our comfort zone.
Laziness	• Takes care of our energy level. • Makes sure the effort we put into something is worthwhile. • Helps us set physical limits. • Without this change blocker, we would be executing every new idea or engaging in everything asked of us, resulting in complete exhaustion. • Patterns of comfort feel good.	• Laziness prohibits us from making healthy decisions. • Often we know what to do, but doing it requires energy and effort that we don't want to expend. • Laziness leads us to believe that the desired result is out of reach. • We do not take the steps to get closer to our goal.
Resignation	• Gives us personal stability. • Helps us accept realistically what we can and cannot do. • Helps us put the human condition in perspective. • Helps us pick our battles. • Without this change blocker, we might lack self-awareness.	• Rigidity prevents us from being open to trying new things or starting new projects. • We are convinced that certain limits are true at all times and in all situations. • We do not dare question old behavior patterns and ways of thinking. It limits our possibilities.

bring. They are collective behavior responses that we all can identify with.

John P. Kotter and Leonard A. Schlesinger (2008) explain that people typically have a distaste for change if they:
- are afraid they will lose something of value
- believe the proposed change has disadvantages or will require too much effort
- are resigned to the current situation.

Let's use the example of John, whose manager is a client of ours. His company is implementing a change program. John is not very enthusiastic about what is expected of him. Those leading the change may interpret this as "John doesn't seem very involved and therefore needs more information." But that isn't necessarily the case. John's change blockers just need a little attention. We need to focus on them, rather than getting frustrated by John's apparent lack of interest.

Three Primary Change Blockers

Once you are aware of possible pitfalls, you can think two steps ahead to predict and prepare for the strategies people will come up with to sabotage change. You can then create plans to overcome them. See the Job Aid, Thinking Two Steps Ahead, for details.

Noni Höfner, a German provocative psychologist, meaning a psychologist whose approach involves playing the devil's advocate, writes that people usually don't want to change their behavior because they find it too risky, too much effort, or too far from their personality. These three barriers can be identified as fear, laziness, or resignation.

These very human pitfalls are ideas that may indicate a fixed mindset as defined by Carol Dweck (2006). People inhibited by these barriers cannot develop their talent to the fullest. In addition, they find it hard to take the step to change.

Change Blockers in Action

Many of our clients wish there were more room for feedback in their organization. They feel that this would be much more positive than a culture where people are hearing information through the proverbial grapevine.

In reality, it's difficult to turn a culture of talking *about* someone into one of talking *with* someone, especially about sensitive behavioral concepts. People don't want to stick their necks out and tell a colleague what they really think. Never mind giving feedback to their boss. People may have had experiences that lead them to believe it's better to say nothing. And sometimes they are absolutely right!

WHY WE CHANGE

Behavior change will occur if:
- a common goal is established
- the desired behavior is mutually agreed upon
- monitoring is organized and executed by all team members
- contracts that state consequences are created
- all those involved accept the human behaviors that get in the way
- those who need extra help receive it
- people are given opportunities to exercise the new behavior
- experiences about successes and failures are shared.

Let's look again at John, the employee who appears unenthusiastic about change. It could be that fear is the change blocker getting in John's way. He is afraid that giving constructive criticism will lead to long-term negative consequences such as loss of favoritism, lack of information, end of friendships, a hostile atmosphere, or retaliation.

> **PEOPLE USUALLY DON'T WANT TO CHANGE THEIR BEHAVIOR BECAUSE THEY FIND IT TOO RISKY, TOO MUCH EFFORT, OR TOO FAR FROM THEIR PERSONALITY.**

Or maybe the change blocker is laziness. He would rather save his energy for things he feels are more important. He may have had experiences in which the effort and discomfort of giving feedback had little or no visible benefit.

Alternatively, it could be that John is resigned to the fact that he is not the type that gives feedback (the third change blocker). He also may feel that the environment he works in is just not receptive to it and never will be. Why bother?

While John does not know for sure that these outcomes will prove to be true, it's not unusual for people to exaggerate negative consequences out of fear. This is what the brain does, and it does it to prevent us from harm (Robbins 1991).

If John were taking part in a change program, these change blockers could impact all of the work he has done to actively change his behavior. For example, during the training he is motivated and recognizes that he should give more feedback because it would be beneficial to the team. He does his best and is encouraged by his colleagues and inspired by the facilitators. He is gung-ho on giving feedback because he has learned a great technique, practiced it, and is still feeling that training high.

However, when he and his colleagues return to so-called real life, the behavioral patterns kick in again, and it's back to where we started. The change blockers are back in play. Many other external factors act as brakes on this progress and definitely need attention. Nevertheless, the internal personal barriers are the key ones to overcome.

DEALING WITH CHANGE RESISTANCE

From our own and others' practice and research, we know that when we recognize the change blockers, accept them, and work with them, rather than letting them work against us, we will have far more success when dealing with or initiating behavior change.

There are several approaches that will help us ensure that we stay on track with change.

Follow-Up

Nearly every change model or method gives us a good overview of the actual situation in the team. We gain insight into how employees communicate, how they process information, and what is important for them. It's a good start—but we are not always consistent in following up on what needs to be done next. Commitment to a structured follow-up strategy is essential to keeping things on track.

Mutual Responsibility

We all know that people need to be motivated and feel responsible for being part of a change. They need to sense both the urgency and the need. Brain science shows that change affects our brain negatively if we do not feel truly involved.

Often, employees can't really be bothered to be part of the change or maintain the momentum because it doesn't feel important to them. They believe that their input is not fully appreciated and that the real change decisions happen elsewhere. Creating true ownership means establishing involvement and input from the get-go.

Ongoing Feedback

From our interviews and work with companies in the Netherlands, such as KLM, the Dutch National Police, and ProRail, we know that programs are only successful when there is ongoing feedback. People need to know what is expected of them, hear how they are doing, and feel the associated consequences. This is difficult to deliver when

AN INSIGHT ON CHANGE

A model or training is usually beneficial because it creates an understanding of the actual situation. However, it rarely gives insight into how to change it and how to organize the change. If you work with a model, you need to build in other phases that help you complete the process. The key is continuous feedback about the behavior you wish to change. As the Dutch say, "Soft healers make stinking wounds." Components such as knowing who you are as a person and what makes you tick are vital to change commitment.
—Hans Raamsdonk, policy adviser, learning and development, ProRail, the Dutch national railway infrastructure

the parameters are not determined beforehand and there is not a consensus on what the desired behaviors are.

CREATING PLANS TO OVERCOME BARRIERS

Behavior change is difficult for all of us. Humans tend to like routine and being in our comfort zone. Why do you think stepping out of your comfort zone has become such a buzz phrase in the learning and development world? If we could do it easily, we wouldn't need a muddy survival course in the mountains with a bunch of ropes and planks to make it happen.

How many times have you started a diet and ended up cheating by eating a bar of chocolate? Or told yourself that you should start organizing your work better? And gotten frustrated that you lost all your documents because you never did back up that system? Sometimes you just don't do what you have promised, not even to yourself.

Change takes time, energy, and attention. This is why it is crucial that change agents have a good understanding of what change actually is, what the obstacles to change are, and which steps are necessary to facilitate the change process. Quick and dirty doesn't work. That is why you as a change agent should be focusing on how you can make it easier for those involved to stick to the plan. Once they have committed, there can be no turning back.

It all starts by creating a vision. This vision needs to be clear to the entire organization, and all members need to understand what it means to them and what is expected of them. Their involvement is crucial. Mutual agreement is key. From this moment on, there is commitment to sustained and sustainable change.

THE C STEPS

We have developed a plan we call the C Steps that, if followed carefully, can promote behavioral change. These steps are based on contemporary neuroscience, interviews with HR managers, an evidence-based parenting program, and elements we've found to be essential in our behavior change programs. The C Steps offer a way to address the circumstances specific to behavior change: follow up, responsibility, and ongoing feedback.

The C Steps are applicable to any change model. In our discussion, we apply them to team change, but you can adapt them to meet your own clients' needs, wishes, and the particular situation.

These are the six C steps:
- Choose
- Consequences
- Control
- Comprehend
- Coaching
- Contributing.

See the illustration on p. 6 for descriptions of the six steps. The job aid at the end of this issue offers tips for implementing the C Steps. Here, we describe each of the steps, offer an example, and share expected results.

THE C STEPS MODEL OF BEHAVIOR CHANGE

Step 6. Contributing
Everyone involved walks the talk. Create a sharing platform, and urge managers to exemplify change.

Step 5. Coaching
Give special attention to those who need more help. Choose a coach and method, with the understanding that behavior change takes practice.

Step 4. Comprehend
Understand the change blockers that prevent humans from changing. Create dialogue, keeping it light by using humor and reverse psychology to talk about obstacles.

Step 3. Control
Make contracts on how to monitor the change process. Set benchmarks on calendar, and encourage curiosity and discussion about the process among colleagues.

Step 2. Consequences
Everyone involved decides on rewards or sanctions for effective—or failed—behavior change.

Step 1. Choose
Change agent encourages clients to determine what specific behavior they would like to see changed.

The C Steps process is cyclical. The steps do not necessarily happen in order.

Choose

Many organizations want a quick fix and will ask you to come in with your "magic wand" and repair everything that's going wrong. The client could have a myriad of issues to cover. For example, they might want to get staff to listen to each other better, share information and knowledge, prioritize their tasks, give more feedback, take ownership and responsibility, manage their clients to increase sales, and in general just be better.

This magnitude of change is just not possible, yet we often say yes to a job like this because we hope that our fantastic techniques will be a panacea. Plus, we like a challenge. We have to stop kidding ourselves and go back to the basics and choose something to focus on. And yet it is difficult to make a definite choice.

Why is that? Remember the change blocker, fear? We are fearful of making the wrong decision and suffering the consequences. So, already during the first step, we are confronted with a change blocker and have to encourage our client to make a choice.

This may be difficult for a client and perhaps for you. An organization's problems are often interwoven. That is why guiding this process is crucial. As a change agent, it is your job to filter through the issues and discover the question behind the question. We do this by probing deeper to really understand the client's basic needs and wishes. These are not just immediate needs of the business but of everyone involved. Often, we use the team's performance goals as a guideline. Behavior that supports these goals is a good place to start.

You need to make sure that there has been at least one session in which all stakeholders agree on what has to be changed. In this session, you will obviously discuss many different areas of concern, but you have to make sure only one or two are chosen for the change effort.

> **THE C STEPS OFFER A WAY TO ADDRESS THE CIRCUMSTANCES SPECIFIC TO BEHAVIOR CHANGE: FOLLOW UP, RESPONSIBILITY, AND ONGOING FEEDBACK.**

Example

Our client, Helen, is the head of an IT staff at the Dutch National Police. When we first met her to discuss her needs, she had a long list of things she wanted to change We helped her filter down her list to one specific theme: giving feedback.

We began with what we call the "miracle" question: If you went to bed with a problem and woke up the next day and discovered that a miracle had happened and your problem was gone, what small change would you see that would make you realize the miracle has happened? This sort of deep interrogation is necessary to guide your clients to choose the one specific behavior they would like to see changed.

But you can't stop here. Once we know what the theme is, we organize a meeting with the whole team to zoom in on the behavior to make it as precise as possible. This takes more probing. What sort of feedback? About tasks? Work attitude? How often should it be given? In what context? How does feedback contribute to your team goals? What will the result look like? Are you sure this is what you want? This step also involves acting as the devil's advocate by making remarks such as, "Come on, nobody will give honest feedback. It will be a farce."

Just asking these questions and playing the devil's advocate can help your clients specify a little more and truly commit to their choice. This specificity will create necessary clarity and granularity. There can be no vague understandings or assumptions. This avoids the problem of someone saying, "Oh, I didn't know you meant that I had to give feedback to my manager," or "Can't I just send an email?"

So we started with the broad topic of giving and receiving feedback, and we drilled down to a specific behavior that everyone agrees on. Every week on the day of the team meeting, sub-teams will meet to evaluate the work processes. Each colleague will ask for feedback and give feedback (a compliment and constructive criticism) to their direct colleagues.

Results

The leader and the team have a clear understanding of what the aims and objectives are. These are the first steps to a mutual agreement. Clients feel like progress has been made because they know that they have made a realistic and obtainable decision. Once these choices are made, people are often relieved because it is tangible and realistic. Now they can begin. The decisions themselves become automatic behaviors. A clear vision brings about the clear objectives that are essential in delivering the intended change.

> **CLIENTS FEEL LIKE PROGRESS HAS BEEN MADE BECAUSE THEY KNOW THAT THEY HAVE MADE A REALISTIC AND OBTAINABLE DECISION.**

Consequences

During this step, we make a contract with the team about what the consequences will be for compliance or noncompliance; we decide how this will be rewarded or sanctioned. Key to this phase is communication. These conversations are straightforward and clear, resulting in written or social contracts that everyone commits to. Rewards and sanctions can be made on an individual basis or for the entire team.

Provocative coaching encourages clients to think outside the box when establishing this contract. Sometimes the craziest way of rewarding effort put into behavior change is just the trigger to get people motivated. This could be fun! Think about what actions will come in handy for your team, what you all will benefit from but just never get around to doing.

Often contracts in the workplace don't work because:
- the behavior is not specific enough
- behavior change is suggested but is not mandatory
- too many changes are happening at once
- the reasoning behind the behavior change is not clear
- the behavioral pitfalls or possible resistance are not considered.

Keep these ideas in mind when developing your contract. And don't underestimate the power of rewarding even small steps. By rewarding all efforts, we rewire the brain to encourage and continue this new behavior.

Example
Let's go back to Helen at the Dutch National Police. Once the contract was established stating that feedback would be given, Helen's team got together and decided on rewards and sanctions if agreements were or were not being met.
- *Sanction*: They decided that anyone who didn't follow up on the agreements would have to give a short presentation on the benefits of giving feedback. Notice that this consequence reinforces the new behavior.
- *Reward*: The team had a night out at a local comedy club. The comedian was briefed ahead of time about the team process and added a few relevant and harmless jokes about, in this case, the police.

Results
Because the entire team decides together on the consequences, there is a critical mass of people committed to and engaged in the process. In

WHAT IS PROVOCATIVE COACHING?

Provocative coaching is on the cutting edge of psychotherapy. In provocative coaching, the coach applies principles from solution-focused (brief) therapy using reverse psychology and warm-hearted humor. Provocative psychology is not simply about telling jokes or making people laugh to make them feel better. It is well-intentioned humor focusing on self-defeating behavior. It can be administered as a method of achieving and maintaining peak performance and has applications in sports and business.

Laughter, humor, and self-awareness are the key ingredients to many success stories of our leaders, managers, parents, and friends. Yet we don't often use these qualities in coaching. Provocative coaching shows that humor is a substantial and even indispensable part of our everyday lives.

Robin Haig, a professor at the University of Michigan, found in his studies on humor that 96 percent of patients felt better if they saw a funny side to their problem, while 94 percent found that humor helped if they were feeling down.

There are five behaviors that the provocative coach wants to instill within a client:
- to increase self-esteem in both language and behavior
- to assert themselves
- to defend themselves in a realistic way
- to behave in a more acceptable social manner
- to overcome reasonable fears.

When provoked in a natural and humorous way, we shake up and shake off unproductive thought patterns. Clients are catalyzed into stating, owning, and enacting the solutions to their problems. The example on p. 10 shows how this dynamic plays out.

addition, the team members let down their guard a bit by having some fun. A serious subject is treated seriously but in a playful way.

Control

Control is about the agreements we make for monitoring and implementing a change process. This step is an ongoing process in which we make sure all parties are playing by the same rules.

You might be thinking, "Control? Isn't that awfully old-fashioned? I work with independent professional people. Why would I need to check on them? Change agents aren't parents or control freaks." But look at it from this point of view. We all need a bit of control in our lives to keep us on track.

The fact that we know that the train conductor may come by to check our ticket encourages us to be honest and buy one. Even though most of us always would do the right thing, being checked up on helps reinforce the choices we've already made. That element of control rewards our efforts and good intentions.

We like to look at control as a ritual. These rituals create settings where people can practice, learn from each other, and keep working on the change. This controlled best practice helps establish genuine role modeling.

Example
The Other Side Movers is an American moving company. The company consists of ex-convicts, recovering drug users, and formerly homeless people. All employees have undergone a two-year program preparing them for employment. The testimonials are outstanding. One typical review effuses, "Wow. This is the best customer experience I've ever had. ... These guys are true heroes!"

At The Other Side Movers, the staff struggled with the same topic our client Helen did. They wanted giving and receiving feedback to be a normal daily activity.

They decided to start giving daily feedback in two ways:
- One is through "pull ups." If you see someone doing something wrong, you are obligated to immediately "pull them up" and then pass the information about the mistake to a crew leader. You don't delve into detail during the pull up—you simply offer corrective feedback. The person receiving the feedback is encouraged to simply respond with "OK." The vast majority of this kind of feedback is delivered by peers—sometimes even a junior peer pointing out a problem to a senior one.

- The second is the "Game." Twice a week, all employees sit in a circle and play the Game. The Game is a peer-driven process of bringing feedback to those you care about and want to see improve. That doesn't mean it is a love fest. It can get loud and raucous. Feedback recipients are often defensive. But as other members of the group add their perspective, those receiving feedback find it difficult to deny the concerns—and eventually they find the humility to embrace what colleagues are telling them. The frequency of Games lowers the emotional stakes over time so that team members become comfortable hearing difficult truths.

Results
You can largely determine the health of an organization by measuring the average lag time between identifying and discussing problems. At The Other Side Movers that lag time is pretty close to zero.

And the results? Ongoing education, no time wasted on repeating the message, and real-time learning. Just in time, just in place, and very efficient. Control mechanisms help people stay on target and remain accountable.

Comprehend

Comprehension of the change blockers is crucial to behavior change. By understanding these change blockers to the fullest, we accept them as a fact and factor them in at the start so we don't waste too much energy on them later in the process. The change blockers become almost so familiar to us so that we can predict possible behavior outcomes. This psychological insight can help us create more efficient programs with a greater chance of success.

First, we need to recognize the positive and negative aspects of change blockers. These emotional strategies have helped us to become

PROVOCATIVE COACHING: AN EXAMPLE

Provocative coaching should always be done in a warm-hearted way. Even though the coach says provocative things, it is never directed against the clients, but only against their self-defeating behavior. The coach provokes direct reactions, and the coachee responds accordingly, triggered to deal with his or her pitfalls. We like to describe this challenging form of coaching as "playing the devil's advocate while being on the side of the angels."

Here is an example of a real-life situation with a manager from the Dutch Ministry of Infrastructure and the Environment, who was not satisfied about the amount of influence he had. He was continuously blaming external factors, for example, his manager.

We noticed that he wasn't exerting the energy to change this situation. This could point to the change blocker of laziness.

The coach uses humor, metaphor, exaggeration, and stereotypes to get the client to assert himself.

EMPLOYEE: My manager doesn't seem to take me seriously. He is always sending me from pillar to post.

COACH: Well, you're not surprised are you?

EMPLOYEE: Why?

COACH: Well, there are two sorts of people: kings and lackeys. You are obviously a lackey.

EMPLOYEE: So you're implying that I do everything he tells me to do?

COACH: Well, do you think you're a king then?

EMPLOYEE: No, but …

COACH: So you're just a loyal servant, or, as I said, a lackey. Simply do what your master says. (*Exaggerated bows*) "Sire, your wish is my command."

EMPLOYEE: (*Chuckles*) They would like that, yes, but there's no way I am going to do that!

COACH: But as a lackey this is exactly what they expect of you. You cannot defy the king's will.

EMPLOYEE: Well, you just watch me!

COACH: My goodness, is this a plot to overthrow the crown? It's surely not at all appropriate for a loyal servant to talk like that! (*Bows again, exaggerated*)

EMPLOYEE: OK, you can stop making fun of me now. But seriously, what I could do is clearly state my ideas and opinions during the next meeting. There is no reason he wouldn't listen. I have led successful projects before.

COACH: Yes, but lackeys just don't do that sort of thing.

EMPLOYEE: Well, it's time that this lackey shows the kingdom what he's capable of.

In the end, the employee asserts himself and expresses what he wants and challenges what the coach says. He can now start to focus on what he can do to exert this new behavior. All of this in only five minutes.

who we are. They keep us from leaning over the desk to choke people who annoy us or jumping into Niagara Falls because it looks like fun. But they also limit us from taking risks and trying out new behaviors.

When the behavior you want doesn't happen—or the behavior you don't want, does—there is always frustration. We beat ourselves up or begin lecturing others. If we comprehend that change blockers are human nature, we can accept that change isn't easy for everyone and recognize how we can help.

Example

Helen was frustrated that her colleagues weren't willing to speak their minds to their peers. It especially bothered her that John wouldn't do it. She saw him as having no drive or commitment and being far too reactive. This prevented her from giving him good feedback about his feedback because she spent too much energy focusing on how he wasn't doing it the way she wanted him to.

We taught her how to "unthink" her previous thoughts and encouraged her instead to embrace John's change blockers and explore the positive aspects of them. This wasn't easy for Helen. It took encouragement, time, patience, and a look at her own change blockers. Once she took a good look at herself, she was able to look more closely at John's change blockers and accept them. This gave John permission to do the same.

> IF WE COMPREHEND THAT CHANGE BLOCKERS ARE SECOND NATURE, WE CAN ACCEPT THAT CHANGE ISN'T EASY FOR EVERYONE AND RECOGNIZE HOW WE CAN HELP.

Encouraging John to "unthink" meant helping him look at his change blockers as if they were a cherished part of himself. We asked him to imagine how he would look at this behavior when he was an old man: What would the older version of yourself advise about your change blockers?

It could be that John identifies with the laziness change blocker. It is his way of saving energy so he can use it on tasks he sees as more integral to his work. Perhaps fear is his problem because, in the past, giving feedback backfired. Or what looks like resignation could be John's realistic acceptance of the way he is.

We encouraged Helen to discuss change blockers with John. She organized a session with John and his colleagues in which they shared their change blockers. One of John's more creative and dramatic colleagues portrayed her fear as a monster hiding under her bed at night. Her monster was quite ignorant, but once it studied up on things, it was able to come out during the day. This colleague's story gave John a model for thinking about his own change blockers.

Results

When change blockers are validated, people stop beating themselves up about their failures and become more accepting. If organizations create dialogue about these human factors, they are no longer taboo. Once teams understand this, they can work on building trust and encouraging vulnerability. All of this will help them to create better solutions for these issues and, thus, obtain their ultimate goal during the change process.

Coaching

During this phase, we work with behavior pitfalls that are more acute and carry greater risks. Coaching is not new, and it is often used during times of change. If much is uncertain and change is constant, individuals increasingly seek out professional guidance to help them navigate the ever-changing waters.

Many people will not need coaching at all because they already have or can acquire the skills and capacities to make the change, especially if all the other C Steps have been addressed. Some people, however, need more support and attention to deal with their change blockers. When a team agrees upon a simple behavior change, coaching is often necessary for those who experience difficulty after trying it a few times.

We define coaching as the International Coach Federation does: "An interactive process to help individuals and organizations develop more rapidly and produce more satisfying results; improve others' ability to set goals, take action, make better decisions, and make full use of their natural strengths" (Bianco-Mathis and Nabors 2014). There are many types of coaching that can help: peer coaching, one-on-one coaching, and on-the-job coaching, to name just a few.

In our practice we use the provocative method, a technique some may see as slightly unorthodox. Provocative coaching uses reverse psychology to trigger participants to take responsibility and ownership. We call it "playing the devil's advocate while being on the side of the angels."

We examine the positive part of the problem to get a complete picture of why the desired behavior isn't yet embedded, even when everyone understands the behavior at an intellectual level. Provocative techniques grab the unconscious brain and shake it up a bit so it can get out of automatic pilot and start to change patterns. The Job Aid, 10 Ways to Coach Provocatively, tells more.

Example
John found it difficult to ask for feedback because of a bad experience with a previous manager. But it was not enough for him to acknowledge the change blocker, fear. The coach helped by stating, in a humorous way, 12 reasons it was good to be fearful of giving feedback: It prevents you from brutally insulting your colleagues, you won't say something wrong and look like a fool, it stops you from ruining the other person's day, and so forth.

John protested by saying that he felt feedback could be helpful in certain cases. He added that he is not always afraid of giving feedback—it's only when he thinks it could affect his career.

By exploring this fear in a coaching session, John felt he understood more about where his fear came from and what was holding him back, and he was able to come up with solutions that felt comfortable for him. All this was addressed in a good-humored, good-natured, and accepting way.

Results
Research underscores the effectiveness of workplace coaching. A 2014 meta-analysis from Tim Theeboom, Bianca Beersma, and Annelies

AN EXAMPLE OF PROVOCATIVE COACHING

Don't give feedback! Everybody knows that they will chop off your head if you do.

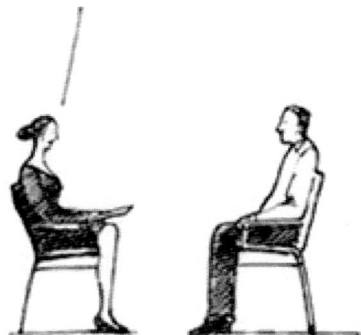

Here, the coach exaggerates the possible consequences to get the employee to speak up against his fear.

Source: Translated from U lijkt mij een vrij hopeloos geval, feiten en misverstanden over provocatief coachen by Adélka Vendl. Zaltbommel, Netherlands: Thema.

E.M. van Vianen shows that coaching can indeed be effectively applied in organizational settings to improve performance and skills, well-being, coping, work-related attitudes, and goal attainment. Provocative coaching ensures a light setting, and the results can be seen immediately.

Contributing

Contributing is all about sharing and encouraging those involved to actively commit to and play a part in the process. This step asks for a company-wide commitment. For managers, it means walking the talk, for example, role modeling the behavior that is to change, despite their own change blockers. There is no point encouraging feedback in the team when managers don't give it to their superiors. It also means managers need to be open to employees' contributions. It's a two-way street where all contributions are considered—whether top-down or bottom-up.

The 70:20:10 principle is based the idea that 70 percent of what people know about their jobs, they learn informally during day-to-day work, with an additional 20 percent coming from relationships with those around them (Henschel 2001). By tapping into on-the-job and relational learning, we can expedite rapid behavior change.

Example
Helen organized a group session in which all team members shared their best practices and experiences. This included what they learned about themselves from their colleagues' feedback, which techniques worked best for them, and the most appropriate time to give or receive feedback.

One team member suggested that they also share their bloopers—the sessions that went wrong, the awkward moments, the good intentions that were never followed through. One person made a short video on his smartphone of how not to give or take feedback. At this point, there was enough trust in the team to encourage vulnerability.

Results
Encouraging contributions gets all members of the company involved. Safe opportunities to practice what they've gained from the process are created and encouraged. We begin to accept and learn from failure. A critical mass of the team becomes engaged and motivated to continue the change process. In addition, the process encourages creativity and proactivity in our colleagues.

ENCOURAGING STAKEHOLDER BUY-IN

The C Steps are a cooperative creation that should involve stakeholders from the beginning and throughout the decision-making process. They see that the change has benefits and that their continued involvement is crucial, necessary, and appreciated. And usually they look forward to participating.

Because we are not relying on a fixed model or technique, we have to ensure that all stakeholders assume ownership and responsibility. But often we forget that for most organizations, the major stakeholders are not management or clients, but the employees on the work floor.

The C Steps inspire creative solutions, not only from the change agents, but also from employees going through it. Giving employees the motivation and tools to drive changes themselves ensures the organization knows where employees want to go and helps them get there quickly and safely with everyone still onboard.

CONCLUSION

Behavior change is tricky. We often hear that change is the only constant in today's market. It will not go away, it will only become more rapid and demand more of employees. They will have to be ever more agile, prepared, engaged, and able to perform to the best of their abilities. That's a lot of pressure. However, employees are certainly capable of all this when given the right attention, autonomy, guidance, and support.

Shining a light on why organizations and individuals resist change won't make the barriers go away, but it will make it easier to get past them. Giving attention to change blockers shows that you take your team's concerns seriously. Let's not make change more difficult than it is. Keep it simple, choose our battles, and have some fun on the way.

REFERENCES & RESOURCES

Books

Duhigg, C. 2012. *The Power of Habit: Why We Do What We Do in Life and Business.* New York: Random House.

Dweck, C.S. 2006. *Mindset: The New Psychology of Success.* New York: Penguin Random House.

Haig, R.A. 1988. *The Anatomy of Humor.* Springfield, IL: Charles C. Thomas.

Hoffner, N. 2010. *Glauben Sie Ja Nicht Wer Sie Sind.* Munchen: Tachenverlag.

Robbins, A. 1991. *Awaken the Giant Within.* New York: Simon and Schuster.

Sells, S.P. 2002. *Parenting Your Out of Control Teenager.* New York: St. Martin's Press.

Sinek, S. 2014. *Leaders Eat Last: Why Some Teams Pull Together and Others Don't.* New York: Penguin Group.

Vendl, A. 2013. *U Lijkt Me Een Vrij Hopeloos Geval.* Zaltbommel: Thema.

TD at Work

Bianco-Mathis, V., and L. Nabors. 2016. "Building a Coaching Organization." *TD at Work.* Alexandria, VA: ATD Press.

Articles

Forman, R.E. 1963. "Resignation as a Collective Behavior Response." *American Journal of Sociology* 69 (3): 285-290.

Henschel, P. 2001. "The Manager's Core Work in the New Economy." *On the Horizon* 9 (3): 1-5.

Kotter, J.P., and L.A. Schlesinger. 2008. "Choosing Strategies for Change." *Harvard Business Review* 57 (2): 106-114.

Stoffer, R. 2002. "Weerstand en Het Dilemma van de Verandering." *Tijdschrift Voor Psychotherapie* 28 (5): 132-141.

Theeboom, T., B. Beersma, and A.E.M. van Vianen. 2014. "Does Coaching Work? A Meta-analysis on the Effects of Coaching on Individual Level Outcomes in an Organizational Context." *The Journal of Positive Psychology* 9: 1-18.

Vendl, A. 2013. "De Kaart Is Niet het Gebied." *Opleiding & Ontwikkeling* 5.

Weeks, W.A., J. Roberts, L.B. Chonko, and E. Jones. 2004. "Organizational Readiness for Change, Individual Fear of Change, and Sales Manager Performance: An Empirical Investigation." *Journal of Personal Selling and Sales Management* 24 (1): 7-17.

Websites

International Coach Federation: www.coachfederation.org.

The Other Side Movers: www.theothersidemovers.com.

Parenting With Love and Limits: www.gopll.com.

Vendl's Provocative Style: www.vendl.nl/provocative-style.

THINKING TWO STEPS AHEAD

The "two steps ahead" practice is a provocative exercise in which team members brainstorm the different ways one could possibly sabotage a change process. Paradoxically, this brings about more trust.

Step 1. Acceptance

Recognize the change blockers. Share some theory about them. Make a collage of your change blockers. Draw a picture. Write a song or poem about them. Ask your change blockers what they need in order to calm down a bit.

Step 2. "Gossip" About Your Blockers

Organize a session with your team in which you all discuss the many ways you would or could not make the change. The manager or facilitator shares first to encourage the process. You could also start in small groups.

Step 3. Talk About the Positive Aspects of the Change Blockers

Take it a bit further and gossip about each other's change blockers. Who has the best way to sabotage this process? "Admire" the sabotaging technique. For instance: "I admire Judy's technique the most. She does not like to be in the spotlight so she just keeps her opinion to herself. She has thoughts about feedback, but she doesn't share them. That way she never offends anyone. Everyone likes that about Judy."

Step 4. Address the Blockers

With the knowledge you've gained, consider strategies you can implement to deal with these sabotage techniques:
- Step back in the past and think about one effective thing you did when this blocker came up and got in the way. Share with each other.
- Take a step into the future and ask the older, wiser version of yourself to give you some advice.

Step 5. Help Each Other and Yourself

Team members decide how they can help address these blockers when they see them. Ask each other, "What can your colleague say to you? What instructions will you listen to?" Make a personal agreement with your change blocker. Ask yourself what you need to overcome the obstacles.

QUICK GUIDE TO IMPLEMENTING THE C STEPS

The C Steps are considerations and concerns crucial to any change program. Implementing all of the steps in a consistent manner will help bring about sustainable change.

Step	Tips to Implement

Choose
 Choose one behavior or learning goal. Make sure the chosen behavior is aligned with the change vision. Be specific.
	• Ask your client questions to understand the need behind the initial concerns.
	 • Allow the client to visualize the desired behavior and results.
	 • Example questions:
	   » What behavior do you want to see and when?
	   » How important is this change to you on a scale from 1-10?
	   » What will happen if you do nothing?
	   » How will you commit to facilitating this change?
	   » Are you willing to spend one hour a day to achieve this?
	   » Is there something more important?
	 • Be patient and don't jump to conclusions. Take your time to make the right choice.
	 • Realize that the change blockers are already playing a role in this process.
	 • Organize a session in which all stakeholders decide on and commit to the chosen behavior.

Consequences Everyone involved decides on rewards and sanctions.	• Organize a brainstorming session around rewards and sanctions. • Encourage everyone to think outside the box. • Choose the ideas that the team relates to the most. • Draw up a written contract and have everyone sign it—this encourages commitment. • Reward small steps.
Control Make contracts on how to monitor the process.	• Set moments in your calendar when you can monitor. • Encourage your client to walk around and see if people are making the change. • Have informal meetings with the client to discuss progress or stumbling blocks. • Encourage curiosity and discussion about the process. • Let those involved decide how they will give each other feedback. • Implement this on a regular basis.
Comprehend Understand the change blockers. Think two steps ahead.	• Create dialogue about the change blockers. • Have people create their own user's guide to their change blockers. • Use humor; laugh about the obstacles. • Talk about how you will most likely sabotage the change. • Come up with viable solutions to combat this sabotaging technique and implement them. • Do failure talks, a five-minute talk in which an employee shares a moment of failure and is rewarded for showing vulnerability.
Coaching Give special attention to those who need it.	• Use provocative coaching for brief and effective coaching on the change blockers. • Behavior change takes practice. Encourage opportunities to implement new behavior. • Organize peer coaching sessions to create understanding, dialogue, and mutual solutions.
Contributing Everyone involved needs to walk the talk.	• Organize a distinct, conspicuous kick-off. • Make the change universal for the entire organization. • Let managers show their team how they are implementing the new behavior. • Have managers share their tips and struggles. • Create a sharing platform for success stories. • Create a safe environment so employees can share their bloopers and other less-than-stellar experiences with each other.